no swaddle

no swaddle

Mackenzie Kozak

University of Iowa Press, Iowa City

University of Iowa Press, Iowa City 52242
Copyright © 2025 by Mackenzie Kozak
uipress.uiowa.edu

ISBN: 978-1-68597-010-9 (pbk)
ISBN: 978-1-68597-011-6 (ebk)

Printed in the United States of America

Design by Nicole Hayward

Printed on acid-free paper

Cataloging-in-Publication data is on file with the Library of Congress.

for Thomas, my love and my light

Contents

"Whether I want kids is a secret I keep from myself—
it is the greatest secret I keep from myself."

—Sheila Heti, *Motherhood*

|||||||

suppose i knew, and held the dogs off

as they circled, and held no swaddle

to my collar, let my hair coat the shoulders,

the arms, or the ancestry, its own bed

carried away, the dark blonde of it.

suppose i faltered at the thought of

startle like a beating hail, blight

of morning, swell to my breasts,

blistered gnawing, and a body warm

with fever and no upletting.

suppose i starved for no truth,

neglecting that wooden room,

so the scent is of hyacinth, and accident,

and i never imagine them.

IIIII

in a room without babbling, i had him

pinned, or he had me in a steel trap, writhing.

there was feather to his soft choking.

but something in me, absent

as an open beak, watching myself

want, up and down with the thigh,

this could be disgust, my twisted nest.

this could be light as the bones of a wing,

to let a thought rise and fall. i had him all

to myself from a lapping of shoulders

and lashes, from a woman who crossed

her feet at the ankles, i had him turning

his neck, scaling my inner wall, in a bed

made of wind and womb.

in a bed made of wind and womb

i began to falter and scatter. half-mast eye,

morning mist that clung until moonrise,

shrugs of cloud hoisting their odd origins

and repetitions. if my mother's mother

had not, then what would not be?

which is also the question of cattle or sheep,

wanting to fill the pen. every day became

a roving tangle of lines, and everyone

asked me to draw the line forward

over an edge. and i said, *what is a line or a hem,*

what if my skirt trails without catching,

can i balance the scale of myself with my own ache,

walking tiptoe through the pine forest?

enter the year with the scowled jaw,

resin in the glass, his ear sometimes

bowed to the moon. the year we suspend

our arms near a wing and collect

unnecessary dread, flies in a jar,

slipping from glass as a spectacle.

what this collecting has made in me

and made off—off and over with

heft to its bite. the year with many

rooms, with hawksbill at dusk,

how the beech leaves did pale

near our gaping. and the jar

which we set in a field gathers

aim, instructing departures.

i was a tired bride, a tired prize.
it didn't hurt the way i imagined.
it didn't hurt like a smart to the head
or a shattered plate, a wall with
its pink gutting, its sulk. i was singing
from the tower tall and shuttered,
i'm so sorry for the new blood on the new
sheet, for the veil to see through, split
to your eye. thought the aisle was
cloud enough, the room of nodding,
then a gasp and quiver. how he lit
the match, his mouth. just a year in
came the questions, *where's the straw*
in your beak, your bulging, that nest?

if i heard you, little heartbeat,
dream of my chest, and could see
your shape strum and heave,
could feel your form shifting,
would i find in me an obscure
passage, an ambling way,
something to counter the course
and inflate it, and to grow it,
and to grow it as one would grow
asters, a leaning, a marveling,
and to grow without remarking
upon the sky, the grasses,
and to grow without pining for
meadows, wind-swept, to rest in.

‖‖‖‖

oh, i can't make a body stay, for it would

have nothing to catch on, to berate,

when mine floats halfway between here

and there. a man tells me, once, *you are never*

fully in view, as i am spread-legged, gnawing

the hide of an apple, thinking of childhood,

of my sister's freckled cheek. or last week,

at the door-screen, the old haunting hitting me,

all the men i have loved have had nooses for eyes,

as i wait for him to make sound, any noise,

scanning the basement for ropes. how to build

upon bodies that fetch themselves and do not

make light work of this, and sometimes lie facedown

toward tombs, and sometimes lie, leaking.

so i carried you off, little spark
of my tongue, banished brooding,
and bothered you with a ledge
to tarry down, winding your wick
northward. but the trickled pink
on the gown, the torn hemming.
so i carried you uphill as battles
shook the ankles and barricades
baited us. i carried you swarmed
in quilting, stinging of heat,
a charred forehead. i drew
marks on a dirt floor to describe
our predicament. i drew closer
to violence, to that still room.

a woman i know who is part-mother tells me, *if you had gotten pregnant at my age, your son would be getting his driver's license.* a sudden speckle to the throat and i am short of breath. i am a nervous driver, a turn too far over the shoulder, jerk to the wheel. i mime a bowing and directing, theater of the wrists, eyes out the back of my head. that night, i dream a baby chokes to death on a wooden table after i feed him popcorn to stop the crying. a dream therapist tells me, *you don't know how to self-soothe.* i tell her, *i don't know how a soothing happens, how a want to soothe arises.* see, everything is a planet or a pushpin, a tire catching black ice in its furrow, a friend of a friend whose story vaults my lung-lock. if i had gotten pregnant at the age a woman inflates to the sound of applause. if i had gotten an earful from nature about my rotting vessel, still, i can't invent a story where i carry the doll from room to room, pausing, *there, there*, with the palm.

love, it is a season of trances,

time of the month, your cheek

a flat hide i try to inflate. you say

there is no pain, no cliff to fret after,

and the windows are sewn shut

in the cave where we drift and devise.

here, pleasure bruises like

a marsh dense with diamonds,

their small sharping, like the stork

of the clock, beak clicking its ring.

in a season of blaring, i shudder

and tear the nails from their walls

so nothing can boast there,

so nothing can tremble or gleam.

he says, *not this year or the next, but maybe*
the next one. the word *geriatric* coats my mouth
like a lozenge, cherry-sharp and gummed. late spring,
cinch to the air, i amass and teethe against
this toss-up, wither each task to its bone,
biting the cuff of it, wallowing, drool of red
sugar and blood. i stare hollow at my figure
and its shoulder, its posture fetal in its curl,
head bowed toward a toughened heel. these years
that do bloom like jaws. i am at the brink of 35
wringing my hands, wringing the towel over
the sink, turning the tap toward a scalding,
and the question that does brace itself
against me is a floating, a ruffle fraying.

and they baited me, drawing
a bridge where a bed should be,
drawing drains where cups
should be. what do i mean?
in the forest he had crumbled
spearmint in his fingers,
let its leaves wilt their odor,
sharp bite to the breath.
and i began to lag behind,
heavy with naming, heavy
as dew drooping a maple's
hand. what i mean is
he kept at one desire
as i strained to see the path.

sometimes i swear in the distance
the coracle, the basket of reeds like
a question, like a hole in the river,
burning a hole through my head,
a sickly floating form. *whose body
was it?* and that was the question,
repeatedly, *whose is it?* and these
questions to turn upstream, to ask
of the figure bowed at her middle,
whose body? when the bending and
the heaving is her own, river of her own
blood, afloat with its sowing. could her body
reign without anchor or raft, its reservoir
intact, and be central to the story?

||||||

mother, i am such a bother, my drift and tear,

mood-making, my raiding of mirrors. in each eye,

a tangle of scrap-metal, shards where a glint should be,

forests of blame. what i took from you i cannot return:

flame in the gut, singing fevers, and a series of coiled scars,

raised like small, silken hairs. what i find in the world

you have fetched me to enter is wheat at my tongue,

and no map to its source, though wind fills my dreaming.

and i can't keep anyone here, can't make them see it,

how you asked me to see, tubes of honeysuckle, inchworms

suspended by fine ribbon, or a cloud when its edge centers

right on the moon's dimpling. how you asked and i did not

say, *no*, through the wilting, scorched heavens, through the years

of the dialing and waking to fever like blood was a sound.

but then there was no one way

to emerge. as in, to tense, to foster

a flame. and no strict echo or thaw.

i took to fanning myself with

feathers, shine to the cheek,

and no wince til i was through

the door. and no wince til i was

through. and the fanning

of paper, of grasses, something

to hold the eye pinned in its pit.

i wanted one way. and he said,

what if there was a center to

move through? and i said, *am i not*

the center through which i move?

i was not a center, i was a spade,

i was a hook dragging on one more

hoggish aim, lightbulb-hungry,

drooling over the lull of the trough.

i wanted hands tied for a pleasure,

race to the pulse. i wanted the spear

of the clock like a dagger to split

me, clean through, or to ask for

the baby, split between us, as a sign

to bow out. or to dig for a mark

that would turn me, wine at the brim

of the tub, musing on doctrine,

sleeping through birdsong, sleeping

through beauty, eye closed to need.

sister, i exhale through my own bandage
and turn from its weeping. a terrible gift,
to feel the flank and fretting mirror.
you asked my mind to lift its mouth
toward opera, nolita, all these higher
notes from underground, and i grew dizzy
in a train car while you held my hair,
just held it, light and heavy as scarves.
it's the arcing that i won't stand, or can't
live through, when we don't know
what's the middle, so the hours are fraught,
bloated fish, and you were born after,
round-eyed, probing *why*, as i walked
reckless toward myself, toward shadow.

||||||

a woman i know who is part-mother tells me,
if he is a good man, you should make more
of him. she means, *he is a good man.* she means,
make more of him. hours later, i am in the bathtub,
touching the pocked bones in my feet, letting
the faucet dim to a whistling, stomach mound
like a small island with a divot in its center.
i want to tell her, *to make anything is to watch it*
eat you from the inside. i want to tell her,
there are days the sunlight is a violence
like a warm bullet, burning its braid through me.
another woman tells me, *there's a mothering*
to knowing what would suffocate you, but
i am never breathing, letting the blight warm me.

i encounter a sort of doom,

set indoors, neat as a pin,

by which i mean it takes up

so little space it can travel

endless distances. by which

i mean it does prick and tease,

bristled nerve, sting and barb

like a tack piercing the skin.

i encounter a doom like a set of

palms, clasping the throat.

i encounter the need to nest

and upend it, and build a structure

to no surmounting, and do not answer

any cries or dream of waking to a call.

||||||

you were on the moon. where
were you? or you had become
a place where the moon appears
beneath the feet. a likely place
for the moon to grow, for its
round punctures. when you left
i had not seen your eyes for hours.
when i saw them again they were
glazed with the moon's glow,
they were grey plates, i wanted
to touch them. i wanted to ask
them where you had been.
where have you been, love?
i was looking up and up.

||||||

i wake from the ruffle and bandage of sleep
and bowl over, clutching the stomach.
and i know what i know—a dry spell in
the sack, no shot at containing—and i know
each blue pill like a seal over something winged,
the self, and still, the faintest thought about
how a term begins in porcelain and nausea.
you're flinching, said a friend, as she described
feeding her son with her breasts. she wasn't wrong.
i wake to illness and sometimes delight in
feeling my own forehead for fever, slicing
my own toast. but i weigh the cost of this against
a blank knowledge, scales that float untethered,
in a room without babbling.

my mother at the throat of dawn, her head

bent in prayer, and a lotion like honeysuckle

steeps each blanket. and her mother, pouring

gin in a coffee mug, setting the table, asking

for a gun to the head, and a glance up to heaven

and a journal entry loosely buzzed and waxing

spiritual, *god, since you are there, absolve me,*

and her mother, from the four-poster bed,

with the desert streams and the moral grounds

for patience in affliction, sickly smell to the house,

and each mother wetting an iron, slicing an apple,

stroking the worn bible pages, their lace, a known

scaffold to sight, a balm, my own mother, what if

there is no finding me in the thread or the split palm?

||||||

broad strokes, i gave you,

wielding the floored hem

of my hair, wielding the forced

air like a gasp in a room

chilled to shivering, clack

and chrome of the vent,

all that unease and quaking

when the need is the voice

to retain a similar decibel,

something to loan when

the word is fraught, when

the word has no end or

its end is an impasse,

an addling, unlaid egg.

i came to you cathedral-mouthed,

a darkened-glass silence to me,

and dug you a theater, a calm dream,

and drank the dredges before a flock

in lit rooms, and guessed at harbors,

concealed them, and came to something

like a swarm, gave reverence to it,

made discourse of it, and wore a robe

that floated as a spirit through the bleating

halls. you gave me heft and gravity,

no float to me, no height or heat,

no wax dripping, no stair to stand from,

and permitted me a rambling row,

to walk down, to warble.

a woman i know who is part-mother

is holding the heel of the phone,

spilling into it, and i emerge without

a crumb to offer. little force field

of the other room, on camera,

reminiscent of blair witch,

is smooshed-cheek in crib corner.

to be all surveillance, or one foot

always elsewhere, i am trying to hover

myself over such ways, to rehearse them,

miming, to sweeten them, to ascertain,

to drift nearer to the shore of them.

to be near in a way that startles me,

hook to the lip, face to face.

sometimes like a haven is another's
rocking, crooning, his claw. in a vision
we are tousled at the tree line, bolt
of sumac as red-rare and the splaying
buttered sourwood. even under shelter,
in the branch's rummage, no one knows
the inside of my clamber, how
my chamber is a trouble in its recess
and its ghost. when we traipse
near shades and feel their pinching,
i grow envy for their gauzy waver,
for their see-through smearing.
he's another in a line of vanishings,
a melting flurry, cloud i don't inhale.

|||||

a mess in oils, greyscale,
from a portrait of myself
on film, 35mm, then tint
and plunge to pigment,
glossy where the figure leans,
where the figure is itself
discrete, itself no vessel
or urn. to bend and shiver
for the sake of psyche not
the sake of sequence.
what's the question? how
did outline form a way
of moving, yellowed harp
of the arm, all only?

i would call her lucy, loulou, little bird. and peel her,

regrettably, from my lush middle, for sleep. lucy,

traipsing through puddles, with the night of my lover's hair,

holding a leaf, as he tells her, *leaf,* telling her, starry-eyed,

of the world. and the dark days, the sobbing, boiled water,

hospital bills on the kitchen counter, not giving

as i was given, striving and falling short. or our moody

shifting, hard to quell or anticipate. lucy, my doll,

mermaid wrung from the water of me, if i have to see

all of it, drawing myself toward you, in order to break myself

from it, spider with eggs in its jaw. if i move toward myself

as an end, not an opening. lucy, could i ask for your love,

for your pardon, if i do not make you? little bird,

could i go on loving myself without this?

moth to a flame, to a mouth:
mother as flare as a flash
in a pan as a high beam
that runs me off-road,
a flume-flooded motor
upturning. or mounting
his frame, all motion
and flurry, motel flicker
of heat. motif with fleas,
with flesh, with the hand
resting mothlike, its fluff,
its mother, flypaper to catch
on. when she flatlines,
no motion, no moat.

sister, everything darkens or splits
to thread. i lay down on the deathbed
of my lover, and i cut his body down.
i am always cutting myself down,
down to the crumb, to the earth's
hacking. in the medieval sense,
i have come to understand the sword
in the frame, the river turning to milk
at dusk, the stars like salmon vaulting
upstream, climbing their bloody
mounds. sister, i am always bleeding
or searching my skin for a wound,
for a bloody star to say what the body
saw and what shape it made in the grass.

or how i deemed myself unfit
to the task. maybe that's the place
to start, for one, i am a woman
who hates to be overheated, hates
to be captured, punching the light
out from the trunk, waving my hand.
and the eye on the cradle, on its rocking,
on the clock, on the nipple, the crumbs
in the car seat, eye on the 10th percentile,
trying to slow my breathing. to be handcuffed
to another, this is not the right way
to think about it, but it is the way i keep
seeing it, peeling myself apart, holding two lives,
one as betrayal, one as a driving off.

stranded by some evening, its round fist,

or doused in the river in the weather

of a stern reckoning. i woke, murmur

and clench, from a dream or a moment

of holding, nose-to-nose, with the call of it,

and grew cameras for eyes, and

took note. and it took me by force

to a want for remedy, overhaul of knowledge,

shell to the ear. how to know as i knew then,

in real time, the want to flee, kick a table in,

or even now, was it that angst, having noticed

the weight of the armor, having knelt

before the woman i hoped to be,

kissing her fingertips, or nodding off.

||||||

i tell you i am so sweet on so
sweet on the baby the baby
out with the bathwater that
slippery wrist slippery head
the sending it all out the water
with it the tepid flat float the
takebacks the trances i'm giving
it all to itself to a distance
i won't travel a distance of brine
the baby its hedging its squall
the damp and driving rain its
coating its holding i sheltered
and shook so sweet when the
whole of it, hand of it, oust.

a back deck increment blinks
cigarette through hedgerow
and a hewn hibiscus. talk
of tender and a seam that's
loosed its yarn, a splitting.
later, lamplight. there's an
unearthed match to scuff
against its grain, to scour
its glow. for a form to surface
like a wraith, its head in
my palm. i retreat and let
the quiver lull, pacing
a stage. pacing a question
with both feet.

||||||

the stage of the mood depends
upon the risk to the body. body
at rest. body at height, in vibration.
body swarming, body a dazed
shade of pink, that sticky flush.
or lower, the arcane growling,
the stowing away, the built husk.
body spreading, socking itself
bruised, body in water, gasping,
treading to pins. i didn't know
mine could run without teaching it,
offering crumbs from my hand,
and my mood hums at a low decibel
but does hum.

mother, this is not the garden you spoke of,

or i have not tended it, as its weeds have grown

waist-high and difficult to wade through.

the man i love grows peonies and does not

blame me for the weather, though he builds cages

to protect the peach trees' faint budding. when the garlic

shriveled and tomatoes bleached with sunspots, i grew

hardened toward the earth. mother, what's the cost

of growing something, or in choosing not to plant,

feeling the wind for an aim. when i was born there,

or you were, when i was a small plot of soil, pressing myself

to your knee. did you wonder what i would become,

or what hours would shape me, what weather, haunt me.

did you move steady through the world, trusting the sky?

||||||

the closeness i wanted. the held and the heat.
but not just any mind with its loose parts,
its cradle. when he walked in a room,
all the matter went out of my head, my mouth
grew arid, and i wanted to lie next to him, in snow,
in the town that raised me, windchill freezing
my hair on the walk to the door. he had me
begging the stars, with god as my witness,
to be near him. see, i have known something
of desire, mounting a body in the swamp-dark,
flooding the room with breathing in a country
of fire. but i have felt nothing of making,
of the small nearness and the leading,
breath on the chest, those purrs.

mother, i comb my psyche for weeds,

little pests, and other marks of untidiness,

until i am encircled by a gleaming resin.

nearby, a magnolia's fanning has eclipsed

to rust, slouching its vessels. but i require

nothing from the landscape, and you

don't speak to me of ivy or the phases

of the moon, even when a neighbor's house

blows nearly off its scaffold, siding pared

to wooden tusks. you are warm inside

the foyer and still shivering. i keep itching

where the rash spreads, asking you why

air funnels and has a mind to slaughter,

what of the robin's eggs, how will i keep clean.

jjjjjj

to go headfirst into such a question,
i must, as i always do, think about
the ending. like the day the ashes
bleached my palms, milk veil in wind,
and their sack a heft of chalk, heavy
as flour, sifting, no rise to them.
and the word i thought was *null*,
was *nothing*, the mosquito on my elbow
clotted red. what's a body in dirt,
down the drain, dusting the fringe
of the dress? where is its shape,
its loom? is the act of birth a scattering?
it was sunset, there were cattle
in the distance, their horns were scythes.

from this patience begets a rattling, murmur

of wasp nest, cloudy inner ear. a man tells me,

beautiful harmonies, when i am not singing,

when i could be stone. and a swarm of them,

raising a tent in the sun's fervor, it takes

so many of them, stretching and pluming a hide,

to lift it, bulge from the earth. all that for something

unbelonging, trees poking up and around.

the reach and the catching, breach and a snagging.

will this patience bend itself to parched edges,

and dissolve into whimpering, a pleading

for certainty, for a structure taller and bright.

i was singing, days after he told me, and

he couldn't hear it, or i couldn't make it rise.

maybe i will call it a juncture

in an effort to abstract it, to hold it

at an arm's length. i am through the roof

and roomy in the blue-blank, dogless,

eyeless in the tree-tread, the warm

meddling. this sweat is shallow

as shell, fraught with whale-teeth,

letting the fray in. and not nearly

razor-sharp, but weighed down with blubber,

or rested as a spoon. but i have swelled

with reason to make haste toward an answer

that will keep me neatly in pocket

in the present, as a line of breezes,

as a towel pressed, nearly, its plush fold.

||||||

sister, what happens at the branching places,

percussive heel, strayed from the source?

decades of our doubling until the tremor

of your neck, its glass. until the tremor of august,

walking around on stilts, dousing the floor.

you knew something i didn't know about waning,

burned lace smearing a room to grey streaks,

swooning to vacuum. i was states away,

painting the body in flight, in a state of repair,

voice a faint crackle of kindling. what happens

to those women, peeling off their coverings.

what happens to those women we carried

to pasture, those smudged mirrors, singed,

sewing themselves with themselves?

IIIIII

a woman i know who is part-mother tells me,
there are second mothers everywhere,
sweeping glass from punctured houses,
dressing the wounds. my lover takes
long spikes to the river and has cleaned
the innards from five trout by late afternoon,
gutted mound of tendrils like the pulsing
worms that caught them. i am searching
a second mother for places where the question
lived and came to a halt, or was gutted
and hung on the hoop of a net, caught
body with the river rushing around it,
a steadying to its drown. i sweep glass
from where a bottle fell. i dress in lesions.

||||||

we watch *red desert* and rocks
are flesh and women fall apart
without a woodstove burning
in a soundless room, quail eggs
on their tongues. his set jaw
and rolling wrist, a tone i know
by rote, is enough to send me
out of frame. which is to say i am
alone again inside the corners
of a keyhole without a ward.
which is to say that i am always
leaning near his sight, wanting
a way out. through an eyelet or
overboard, leaking old fire.

lucy waking, clutching the fence of the crib,

holding a rattle to her red gums. lucy with fistfuls of grass,

sporting a scraped knee, high-pitched wailing.

lucy riding a bike, a skateboard, driving a car too fast

near the curb, lucy drifting through classes, drawing

cartoon tigers, joining choir, soccer, trying out for the play,

or coming home to stare blankly at walls. lucy in therapy,

on prozac, popping adderall, flushing pills, staying clean,

meeting a man who worships her, a man who hits her,

a woman whose skirt grows damp from the dew.

lucy in and out of love, in and out of work,

trying for grad school, a new york apartment,

acquiring debt, breaking even, lucy asking for help,

her laugh through the phone, her faint whisper.

mother, i pair your ardor with wonder
and wrought-iron blooming. we spoke
of doors pinched by daylight, their scour
and scale, as we surveyed a rift. and
you praised ruth at a man's undersole,
making way for a son, your mind strewn
with fissures for flares to drift in. i make
way for a sulking and humor your tablet,
your lifting, when i could lie anywhere,
fawning, and still fumble the mark.
mother! gates do me in, their push-pull,
their hinting at bounds. i snare myself
with them and squint at my slagging.
my furnace is blank and lukewarm.

i have a way of being stepped on when
i aim to please, of being jostled. my lover
dunks his palm into a wash of painted fern
and shakes it, and a crowd of hosta goes faint
near his touch. at a gathering of folk musicians,
a man lectures me on how to be a woman worth
staying faithful to, which includes mastering
the bass guitar and other physical acts. i stare through him,
toward a willow whose limbs like wet hair absorb and produce
beads of rain. i want to be a good woman, i think,
unless it means attention to clocks, to dials, dragging
a finger over the mantle, smoothing a crumpled skirt.
but what else could i mean? the willow swings
its heavy strands, shakes itself, does not upend or howl.

mother, all things are heaven or

they aren't, aren't they? things of

the sky, ferried. things of the soil,

sprawled. i was one or the other:

volunteering, kneeled, or bleeding

out on the sidewalk. he says, *you have*

so many rules, and i say, *each page*

bears a context, decomposing, as i

tremble about. he says, *everything*

is a pedestal, a stairway, and i say,

everything stills from this perfect height.

everything is a bore or a bent brow, all flitting,

or suffering. mother, you had a soothing

for any ail: your cloak, your roof.

llllll

and the women around me, my sirens,

flame and delight, grow doubled and weary,

the seep before the wading in, and everything

is siphoned or whittled down to the most practical:

machinery, cotton, metal pails. they build sacks

of liquid while i follow gravel roads to mountain rivers

where the water shocks my body numb, over and over,

ducking into that velvet when the static returns to

fingertips. there is something here, i know it,

about grief and envy, webs i am caught in,

or the passage through layers and pebbles,

sifting for junctures. or the dream that we might

all remain daughters, drifting, clutching our hands

together, chanting through fog, warping the way.

IIIIII

a couple of orgasms before noon, work

of my hand. and coupled frenetic as a puzzle

as the riddling of doubts. the fury i tread toward

and then recoil from, pulse of the palm. i rotate

the cuff of my chin, of that chain, to examine

a blade, then denounce it. and drag a finger

through the fever of his mind, while the yarrow

un-yellows itself, crisps to chrome. and what

am i drumming up, some would say, and to that

i would rotate the blinds, hemming and hemming

my heel. a couple of absences, one by choice,

one with the shock of a blight, a few spots

and nowhere again to unfurl. and all this

in the sharp light of day, as if blessed.

‖‖‖

or what of the ending,

the pinch-pulse, hood-flutter,

glove at the ready? who to marvel

in the morgue, ensue the weeping?

there is a solitary boneyard near

a meadow where my slippers

patter, where the lifeblood slows

its purr. without her, no one

ushers me there, no braid to

the arm, and my flatline is

a trapping that i stitched

with vein. i imagine floating

freely, that easy slipping, or

an ache to idle at the gate.

a woman i know who is part-mother tells me,

it's what i was born to do. i look at my hands,

tense my ankles. *born*, to be fastened to

a wound string. to a silken bulge, a steeping,

gelatin quake. like some want to be expelled

as fingers prime and tense. tell me how.

sometimes doing is one daily task and i cannot take it,

when the morning starches and fails me, its strands

strangling. or i give more that i can grant myself

to ask for. or my words dissuade me, or hound me.

what was i born for, or what would i bring here

with that intention, if that one is a pool of mud,

a street, a stubbled mound. i'm no martyr.

i want cushions where my head goes.

||||||

sister, scent is a marker, a marigold

pitching its fit, its musk. his body

mounting a bluff, catching that climb

to swell, to unpocket. i mention

the mood of the valley as mammoth

and glazed in the flood, as the mind,

sunken and eager to spill. mine does

hardly without any hinging, needing

an urging, as you call me, injured,

and speak of the heat. as i reach

through buildings to float you,

weightless, unknowing. your head

as an infant was damp sweetgrass,

its warm dough, its plume.

a woman i know who is part-mother asks me,
what will you do years from now, when
his longing incites a bitterness? and i tell her,
his urge is plaited and far-off, away and apart
from me. we are gloveless in winter, and she
straightens the knit cap on her daughter's head,
and i pinch my fingers into *o*'s. i want to ask her,
how do you know what will and will not incite
a bitterness, or *what is it about his longing*
that excludes my own body, my torn innards,
my breached rounding, but i say, *she is so sweet*
and small, her eyelashes are delicate hooks,
when you see her can you see yourself, can you see
yourself, will you see me, if i do not follow suit?

|||||

love, the thought enters my mind
like a fraying spool of smoke, fuzzy
at the field and the curl, the letting
of rings. and should there be more,
a wreck of things, to place between us—
a doll, a cotton tide, to fracture?
we who have welcomed sound like
the back of a hand, like a steel trap.
we who have welcomed warm mounds
with a shudder and wince. and should
i have welcomed it, beat and bellow,
as snow, to cover and silence me,
to lose track of my throat? the self
as bark as a branch to break off?

IIIIII

i give it a week, a month, four years,

fifty-one scrapped quiltings. i give it

the hive of my skull, thoughts like

thrummed bees, a drowsy panting.

and the eyes and the ears, all their

admissions, the caught kite, jolt

of a slide, leaked juice box, new-legged

staggering. and the implication

of days like long threads to be strung,

ribbon of may day, peeled apples,

feet poised on pegs of a bike. i give it

almost the length of a life, in its

spooling. and the nothing like an itch,

the mosquito on my elbow clotting red.

so what we have come to, says, *childless*,

says choking the throat of the lineage,

shedding its veined ribbon, its seep.

goodbye the chin-cleft, the bulbed triceps,

his burnt umber hair, its soft sheen, and mine

like a curtain of grain, our eyes big as barrels

in the evening, collecting their pangs,

collecting their ruins like small statues,

lining them up for the moon to see. goodbye

that room i grew even before the cord was cut

and my throat filled with noise, that room nearly

ridding itself, red quince flowering in rain,

all the torment and trace of it, as we taper

to no echo and no shadow and no line.

what does it feel like? to chase without
scent, in a foreign landscape, a certain
expiring, or to be made of glass bottles,
shipless, rudderless. *what are you after?*
some semblance of a good life, an omen,
a pitchfork, blank lineage, taste of moss,
freely. *and what would that give you?*
a choice to untangle from the mother,
to hold myself, to unharm. *will they
let you?* each letting is a pursed lip,
blunt sword at the throat, asking for
proof of intention, asking for something
of equal ounce. *will he let you?*
he is a prairie staged uphill, squinting.

IIIIII

and how did we come upon it,

the muscle of another parlor?

bed hooks hoarse and lunging

do not pry me open, bellow of

wolfhound does not arrest me,

tearing drapery, tripping my gait.

when he calls me *milkmaid*,

in the pool hall, under a quivering

light, there are ruffles to his teeth.

i am tying an apron's ribbon a shape

like ceaselessness, flimsy and opaque,

closing and opening an aperture.

when he calls me *milkmaid*, i exhibit

one marshed eye.

after all this, the riddles, the deep and flowered

visualizations, brushed hellebore, wounded hours

with my lover on a velvet couch, misting, trying

to calculate some kind of ruin, after the score lifts

the strings to a soft hovering, and we note the graphs

with their stern etchings, after the foil around the grapes

and the sighing, the standing in the fridge's dull wind,

after wild turkey on the porch of a cabin, combing

for streetlights, hounds circling loose firewood,

after my eyes darting to each stroller for hands,

clutching, studying a woman's face like a ledger,

after the grief and the other grief, the one that goes

translucent if you stare too long, years of this

and i'm still thinking of myself.

Acknowledgments

I would like to thank the editors of the following journals in which these poems (or earlier versions of them) first appeared: *berlin lit* ["love, it is a season of trances,"]; *Colorado Review* ["a woman i know who is part-mother tells me,"; "mother, all things are heaven or"; "sister, i exhale through my own bandage"]; *On the Seawall* ["so what we have come to, says, *childless*"]; *Missouri Review* ["but then there was no one way"]; *Muzzle Magazine* ["after all this, the riddles, the deep and flowered"]; *Thrush Poetry Journal* ["a woman i know who is part-mother tells me, *if you had gotten pregnant*"].

With immense gratitude to my teachers for their wisdom, encouragement, and attentiveness throughout my writing journey—David Biespiel, Frank Burns, Conor O'Callaghan, Jim Clark, Stuart Dischell, Jim Hans, Terry Kennedy, Ellen Kort, David Roderick, Elisabeth Whitehead—and to the Department of English at Wake Forest University and the MFA program at University of North Carolina at Greensboro.

To my writer friends who have inspired me and brought laughter and keen eyes to the strange business of making—Ann-Marie Blanchard, Beckie Dashiell, Molly Sentell Haile, Luke Hankins, Kerry Anne Harris, Catherine Hawkins, Abigail Lee, Cory MacPherson, Mike Pontacoloni, Lauren Smothers, Eric Tran, Brit Washburn, Corrie Lynn White—and to Punch Bucket Lit and the Asheville poetry community.

To the writers who have gone before me and paved the way for language that startles and upends: Lucie Brock-Broido, Feng Sun Chen, Darcie Dennigan, Louise Glück, Sheila Heti, Joanna Klink, Maggie Nelson, Michael Ondaatje, and Diane Seuss.

To the writing residency at Weymouth Center for the Arts and Humanities, where many of these poems were written.

To Brenda Shaughnessy for finding something of value in these pages, Jim McCoy for your direction in this publishing process, Susan Hill Newton and Elizabeth Sheridan-Drake for their editorial direction, and to all the staff at the University of Iowa Press for their attention and care.

To my therapist, Jesse, who witnessed my process of grappling with the questions addressed in this collection and helped me find the freedom to write these poems.

To my family: the Connellees, Allens, Kozaks, and Riccios, all of whom care deeply for language and lyric. To Melanie, Lee, and Morgan, the original loves of my life, for their fierce support and presence. And especially to Franny, my refuge, and to Thomas—my favorite poet and musician, my best and first reader, the most tenderhearted man I have ever met. Our life together is my greatest gift.

To an inclusive and affirming God, for the courage to love anything at all.

Finally, thank you to anyone who is sitting in the cloudy spaces of grief over how to live a life.

IOWA POETRY PRIZE AND EDWIN FORD PIPER
POETRY AWARD WINNERS

1987
Elton Glaser, *Tropical Depressions*
Michael Pettit, *Cardinal Points*

1988
Bill Knott, *Outremer*
Mary Ruefle, *The Adamant*

1989
Conrad Hilberry, *Sorting the Smoke*
Terese Svoboda, *Laughing Africa*

1990
Philip Dacey, *Night Shift at the
   Crucifix Factory*
Lynda Hull, *Star Ledger*

1991
Greg Pape, *Sunflower Facing the Sun*
Walter Pavlich, *Running near the
   End of the World*

1992
Lola Haskins, *Hunger*
Katherine Soniat, *A Shared Life*

1993
Tom Andrews, *The Hemophiliac's
   Motorcycle*
Michael Heffernan, *Love's Answer*
John Wood, *In Primary Light*

1994
James McKean, *Tree of Heaven*
Bin Ramke, *Massacre of the Innocents*
Ed Roberson, *Voices Cast Out to Talk
   Us In*

1995
Ralph Burns, *Swamp Candles*
Maureen Seaton, *Furious Cooking*

1996
Pamela Alexander, *Inland*
Gary Gildner, *The Bunker in the Parsley
   Fields*
John Wood, *The Gates of the Elect Kingdom*

1997
Brendan Galvin, *Hotel Malabar*
Leslie Ullman, *Slow Work through Sand*

2015
John Blair, *Playful Song Called
    Beautiful*
Lindsay Tigue, *System of Ghosts*

2016
Adam Giannelli, *Tremulous Hinge*
Timothy Daniel Welch, *Odd Bloom
    Seen from Space*

2017
Alicia Mountain, *High Ground Coward*
Lisa Wells, *The Fix*

2018
Cassie Donish, *The Year of the Femme*
Rob Schlegel, *In the Tree Where the
    Double Sex Sleeps*

2019
William Fargason, *Love Song to the
    Demon-Possessed Pigs of Gadara*
Jennifer Habel, *The Book of Jane*

2020
Emily Pittinos, *The Last Unkillable Thing*
Felicia Zamora, *I Always Carry My Bones*

2021
Emily Pérez, *What Flies Want*

2022
Melissa Crowe, *Lo*
Maggie Queeney, *In Kind*

2023
Stephanie Choi, *The Lengest Neoi*
Peter Mishler, *Children in Tactical Gear*

2024
Mackenzie Kozak, *no swaddle*
James Shea, *Last Day of My Face*